GW00499539

GOLD PRODUCTION
FROM BEGINNING TO END

WHAT GOLD COMPANIES DO TO GET THE
SHINY METAL INTO OUR HANDS

MARIUSZ SKONIECZNY

INVESTMENT PUBLISHING
MISHAWAKA, IN

Mariusz Skonieczny/Investment Publishing
1202 Far Pond Circle
Mishawaka, IN 46544
www.classicvalueinvestors.com

Ordering Information:
Quantity sales. Special discounts are available on quantity purchases by corporations, associations, and others. For details, contact Investment Publishing at the address above.

Gold Production from Beginning to End/ Mariusz Skonieczny. —1st ed.
ISBN 978-0-9848490-1-7

Table of Contents

Acknowledgments

I am grateful to several individuals who helped me with the book. I would like to thank Peter J. Hawley, Manuel Gomez Rubio, David Landy, Robert Baldock, Paul Noland, Jerry Huang, and Sunny Pannu for reading the manuscript and providing me with invaluable feedback.

Preface

Preface

AS AN INVESTOR AND newsletter writer, I have studied hundreds of companies in many different industries. What I found shocking is how little investors know about the gold mining business. It is mind-boggling.

As Jim Cramer from Mad Money would say, "They know nothing." When I say this, I don't mean some mom-and-pop investors, I mean analysts from big funds controlling billions of dollars of investable assets. They truly have no idea how this business works.

If you don't believe me, then call a few mining CEOs and they will tell you. One mining executive that I became good friends with told me that these investors are nothing but armchair CEOs. They sit in front of their Excel® spreadsheets shouting orders and telling you how incompetent you are when you don't deliver a certain amount of gold production per quarter. They think that starting a mine is like flipping a switch.

Another mining executive told me through e-mail communication, "It's amazing how many people I met who are part of big funds and how little they know about mining...ridiculous!!!"

As a result of other investors' lack of understanding, you can make and lose a lot of money investing in gold mining stocks. You might wonder, "If I know more about gold mining than other investors, how can I possibly lose money?" Well, because if the majority of gold mining investors are ignorant and they control the trading of these securities, your stocks can be down significantly in the short- and medium-term even though you might be right.

However, when the pendulum swings deeply into negative territory and gold mining stocks are trading for pennies on the dollar, you can make an absolute killing if you are positioned properly because of your knowledge.

As I am writing this book, the gold mining industry is extremely hated. It is so hated that some gold mining companies are trading at such levels that when the industry turns, there will be 20-, 30-, and even 100-baggers all over. In other words, a $10,000 investment can turn into a million.

The purpose of this book is to educate you about the gold mining business by teaching you the basics. It will not make you an expert, but it will give you the foundation from which you could become an expert if you want to. With this knowledge, you will be able to pick up an annual report or press release from any gold mining company and actually be able to read and comprehend it. Then, you will have a shot at valuing the mining companies properly instead of just listening and relying on other investors who may not know what they are doing.

People have been fascinated with gold for thousands of years. Many dedicated their lives to the search of it. Some even were killed because of it. At some point, gold also served as official money.

Today, gold is not as widely important as it was many years ago. To some, it still represents money while to others, it is a shiny commodity with little use. Whether you are in one camp or the other, one thing is indisputable – over long periods of time gold maintains its purchasing power.

In 1972, the price of gold was $38 per ounce, and today, it is $1,140 per ounce. I can almost guarantee you that in 50 years, the price of gold will be higher than today. I am saying that not because gold will appreciate in value. It is because central banks around the world will cause currencies to depreciate over time.

You see, gold did not appreciate from $38 to $1,140 per ounce. It stayed the same. It is the US Dollar that depreciated by so much during that time period. As long as governments and central banks continue to act like governments and central banks, all the currencies will always depreciate in relation to gold. Yes, over short periods of time, they will fluctuate and even appreciate in relation to gold, but over long periods of time, paper currencies will move in one direction only – down.

As a result of this dynamic, there will always be demand for the shiny metal and the gold mining industry will have to satisfy that demand. This book will take you on a journey of gold production from exploration and mining to processing and refining.

[1]

Exploring

[1]

Exploring

IF YOU STEP BACK and look at gold production, the process appears to be pretty simple. You find the deposit, dig it out of the ground, sell it, and get rich in the process. The problem, of course, is to go through this process profitably. In other words, the cost of finding it and digging it of the ground must be less than the final sale price to the end customer. This chapter is about finding the gold.

We've all seen numerous Western movies where a character would prospect for gold with a pan in the river. Have you ever thought about why he had a pan and why he was panning in the river?

Gold is a chemical element with the symbol Au, which can be found in the periodic table of elements that some of us struggled to learn in high school during chemistry classes.

Periodic Table of the Elements

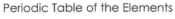

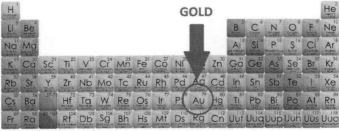

While there isn't complete agreement among scientists about the origin of gold, we do know that it is widespread in the Earth's crust. During the formation of the Earth, many gold deposits developed.

In general, gold is found in two types of deposits: lode deposits and placer deposits. They are referred to as primary deposits and secondary deposits, respectively. Lode deposits are the original gold formations within the rocks of the earth. These types of gold deposits are extremely difficult (read expensive) to extract. Lode deposits are the kind of deposits that commercial mining companies work with.

Placer deposits are the derivatives of lode deposits. In other words, placer deposits are lode deposits that have broken away from their original locations because of water, erosion, wind, earthquakes, thunder, or even mankind.

Placer deposits are the kind of deposits that have been worked and prospected by individuals. Think "person" when you think of placer deposits. Commercial companies usually do not work with placer deposits because they are very hard to quantify.

Individual prospectors go to rivers to find gold because they rely on nature and physics to help them find it. Once gold ends up in water, especially in rivers, it moves with other rocks. However, because gold is heavier than other rocks, it tends to sink to the bottom. Consequently, it can get stuck between rocks at the bottom or at bends in the rivers.

Specific gravity is the ratio of the density of a substance to the density of water. Gold has a specific gravity of 19.3 (density of 19,320 kg/m³) meaning that it is 19.3 times heavier than an equal volume of water. So, water has a specific gravity of 1.0 (density of 1,000 kg/m³). Quartz has a specific gravity of 2.65. Lead has a specific gravity of 11.3. When gold is mixed with other metals in the river, water separates it from everything else and this is how prospectors can find it.

Next time you read in an annual report of some mining company that is using a gravity circuit, you should know that the whole process is about separating gold from other minerals by using its gravity characteristics.

The same applies to panning. Prospectors place gravel in the pan in the hope that gold is present. Then, they add water and shake. They shake so that the heavy gold sinks to the bottom or collects on the pan's edges.

RIFFLES TO CATCH GOLD

Now, let me turn toward lode deposits because these are the kind of deposits that mining companies work with. They are the kind of gold deposits that remain locked within their original solid rock formations. To extract them, you need expensive sophisticated equipment that is much too expensive for individuals to obtain. Usually, if individuals want to be involved in lode deposits, they mainly focus on finding them. For example, a couple of geologists may get together to form a prospecting or exploration company. However, once they find a commercial lode deposit, they will normally try to sell it to a well-funded mining company capable of developing it.

Because developing lode deposits into commercial mines is capital intensive, not all them can be turned into mines. Actually, only one in 3,000 discoveries is turned into a mine. In other words, the well-funded mining companies are extremely selective about which gold projects fit their acquisition criteria. This is because huge amounts of money are involved and the input costs must be less than the expected revenues in order to generate profits.

How are commercially viable gold deposits found? They are found by physically drilling holes in the ground in order to obtain samples that are later analyzed for gold content.

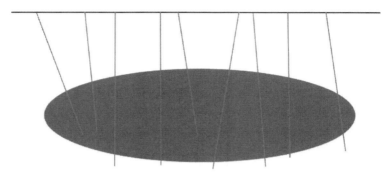

If the black horizontal line is the land surface and the rounded shape is the gold deposit, a gold exploration company can get a pretty good idea of how large a particular deposit might be by drilling holes through it. The closer the holes are to each other, the more precise and reliable the estimates.

WHERE TO DRILL

The reason why gold mining is such an expensive endeavor is because every step of the process takes a significant amount of capital to complete – one million here, two million here, and a hundred million there. It is no different when it comes to drilling. Drilling one meter into the ground can cost as much as $200 or more. During periods when drilling contractors are busy, the cost per meter is high and when they are idle, the cost per meter is low. Either way, drilling is expensive. Diamond drilling, which I will discuss later, is particularly expensive. For example, a mining company performing a 30,000-meter drill program can spend between $3 and $6 million just to drill a bunch of holes. And, this does not mean that they will find enough gold in the ground for the deposit to be economical. I hope you are getting a sense of why the exploration business is so risky.

Because drilling holes can make millions of dollars disappear quickly, decisions about where to drill are not taken lightly. A lot of times, companies will drill in areas that are adjacent to or near other gold discoveries. It makes sense because gold deposits can extend for miles and if there is a discovery in one area, there might be another one a little bit further in either direction.

For example, I recently wrote about Oroco Resources for my investment newsletter, Ultimate Value Finder. Oroco is a tiny exploration company that owns Xochipala Gold Project, which is located in the well-known Guerrero Gold Belt in Mexico where more than 30 million ounces of gold have been discovered. This project is among the last known underexplored geological structures in the region.

Because of its proximity to other successful gold discoveries, the company is getting ready to embark on a drill program in the hope of making a meaningful discovery. If they are successful, the kind of money that investors can make is mind-boggling. If they find two million ounces of gold in the ground, which is what they hope for, then this is equivalent to $2.3 billion worth of gold, assuming the price of gold is at $1,140 per ounce. From that amount, all kinds of costs have to be subtracted, such as development costs. However, considering that the company's market cap is only $2 million, there is significant upside. If you want to see my report on Oroco, go to www.goldminingbook.com/oroco

The mining companies can also drill in areas where gold mining took place years ago. We have all heard of ghost towns that were once booming towns but were later abandoned after the economic gold was depleted. However, with a higher price of gold and enhanced extraction technology, those old deposits might be economical again.

Today, mining companies are desperately looking for new gold deposits. Consequently, they often revisit the old workings in the hope of finding economical gold that was left behind in the ground. Also, what the old-timers might have considered lower grade before might now be classified as high because, let's face it, everything is relative. Back then, the deposits that we are mining today would not even be considered because the price of gold was too low to make them economical. With that being said, there were a lot of high-grade deposits available, which is not the case today.

Other places mining companies explore for gold today are previously inaccessible areas. Geologists are like detectives. They look for clues and signs of where gold can be hiding. For example, gold can appear with copper and lead. Therefore, geologists look for the presence of these other metals in the hope that there will also be gold. The problem for geologists today is that the Earth has been scanned for gold so many times that the easy-to-find gold has already been claimed. However, there are areas that were previously inaccessible and now, with new drilling technology, they become accessible.

In the gold mining industry, the traditional drill rigs are truck-mounted, which means that they need roads to access the deposit. One company that I own stock in is called Energold Drilling. Energold used to be an exploration company that faced problems with exploring hard-to-access areas because traditional rigs were truck-mounted. To solve this problem, the company developed its own "man-portable" rigs which can be disassembled, carried by people, and reassembled on site. This technological advancement allows mining companies to drill for gold in areas where they were not able to drill before. I encourage you to watch the following YouTube video about Energold Drilling to get a sense of what I am talking about.

Mining Industry TV Clip on Energold Drilling (EGD: TSXV)
www.goldminingbook.com/energold

What about drilling for gold in areas that do not offer any clues of a gold presence or areas where previous miners were unsuccessful? This is called greenfield exploration. Exploration in areas with known gold occurrences, as I discussed in the previous paragraphs, is called brownfield exploration. As you can imagine, brownfield exploration is less risky because there are more clues present while greenfield exploration is the riskiest type of exploration. Exploration companies are often categorized as either greenfield or brownfield exploration companies. Greenfield exploration is also called grassroots exploration.

In order to determine whether an unexplored area is worth drilling, various scientific studies can be employed. They may include geological, geophysical, and geochemical studies. Geophysics and geochemistry are subdisciplines of geology.

Geologists may start by looking at geological maps in order to find promising areas to explore. Then, they may use geophysics and geochemistry to narrow down their searches.

Geophysics is the scientific study of the Earth's internal structure dynamics by using physics and mathematics. For example, the Earth's crust consists of different rock materials which have different physical properties such as density, magnetization, and electrical conductivity. Consequently, if you can map out certain areas based on density or magnetization, you might get clues as to whether gold might be present.

The aeromagnetic survey is a popular type of geophysical survey conducted by flying airplanes at a constant altitude. A magnetometer is attached to the plane and it measures the total intensity of the magnetic field generated in the earth. When the survey is complete, aeromagnetic maps are produced with different colors representing the different magnetic energies produced by different rocks.

While using this method allows exploration companies to cover large areas in short periods of time, the obvious drawback is that the maps can only show the geological structure of the upper levels of the Earth's crust.

Another geophysical study is called gravity survey. This technique uses a gravitometer to measure the density of different rock types and map them out with different colors like the aeromagnetic maps.

Remember how in the previous section I talked about gold's density and its specific gravity of 19.3? Well, different rock types have different densities, and gravity surveys measure them. This gives geologists and geophysicists a picture of the sub-surface geology of a surveyed area.

Watch this YouTube video.

Gravity Surveying

www.goldminingbook.com/gravitysurveying

Seismic surveys are also geophysical studies that help determine the composition of the rocks beneath the surface. Seismic studies involve generating subsurface vibrations by either hydraulic vibrators or explosions to generate seismic waves to penetrate the underground surface. In other words, seismic studies involve creating small earthquakes in order for the underlying rocks to give off sound that is picked up by microphones called geophones which are located on the surface. All the data is compiled to create seismic maps which are nothing but sound pictures of what is beneath the surface. While seismic surveys can be used for gold exploration, they are extremely popular for oil and gas exploration.

Geochemistry is a science that uses chemistry to understand the geology of the Earth's crust. By knowing the chemical composition of rocks, mining companies are able to get clues as to whether a gold deposit might be present.

Geochemical studies may be conducted during the gold exploration process along with geological and geophysical surveys. Geochemical surveys include collecting and analyzing samples of soil, water, debris, and plant tissue to understand their chemical makeup. In the past, geochemical studies were not used in gold exploration, but by 1970, they had become an integral part of mineral exploration for gold and other metals. The reason why they became popular is because studies proved that most metallic mineral deposits leave traces of their chemical composition in adjacent and enclosing rocks. Because of weathering, which is the breaking down of rocks, soil, and minerals, they also leave chemical traces in materials such as glacial sediment, soil, and spring or stream water.

How to Drill

After the decision is made about where to drill, mining companies can embark on their drilling programs which will unveil what is hidden under the ground. Drilling defines the size and quality of the deposits. Eventually, this information is included in a National Instrument (NI) 43-101 technical report prepared by an independent third-party engineering firm, which is unbiased.

If you have ever studied a mining company, you have probably heard of exploration drilling versus production drilling. In this section, we are talking about exploration drilling which is used to define a deposit. Production drilling occurs during gold production.

There are many types of drilling techniques and they all have advantages and disadvantages. One method might be the cheapest but not the most accurate. Another method might penetrate the earth the deepest but may also be the most expensive. Either way, the purpose of drilling is to get samples that can be analyzed and studied for their gold content. There are two basic types of drilling methods. One type produces rock chips and the other type produces core samples.

Auger Drilling

Auger drilling is the cheapest of the cheap drilling methods. It only penetrates up to 25 meters into the ground. This method uses a helical screw which is driven into the ground through rotation.

 Auger drilling is mostly used for soft ground because it would fail to penetrate extremely hard rocks. Often, it is used in conjunction with the geological, geophysical, and geochemical studies that we discussed in the previous section.

RAB Drilling

RAB (Rotary Air Blast) drilling is the next cheapest, but it is a bit more penetrative than auger drilling. Therefore, it is typically the first step in the mineral exploration process. It costs as little as $6 per meter, but it goes only as deep as 150 meters. This drilling technique is also known as Down-The-Hole drilling because it uses a mini jackhammer on the bottom of a drill string. A drill string is the apparatus comprised of drill pipe and drill collars that links the drill bit to the part of the tool that creates the drilling motion, which is either percussion or rotary. Compressed air is used to power the hammer into the ground to break the hard rock into smaller pieces. The broken rock is then removed to the surface through a narrow space between the drill rods and the side of the hole. Because it is hard to visualize RAB drilling through written words, watch the following two YouTube videos.

Air Rotary Drilling
www.goldminingbook.com/airrotarydrilling
Down the Hole Drilling Method
www.goldminingbook.com/downtheholedrilling

RC (Reverse Circulation) Drilling

RC drilling is more expensive than RAB drilling but it is also more penetrative. It penetrates up to 500 meters and it costs between $30 and $45 per meter. This drilling method was developed in Australia in the early 1970s.

RC drilling uses dual wall drill rods with an outer tube and inner tube. The cross section of the drill rods showing both tubes looks like this:

Inner Tube

This rod is connected to the drilling head called a drill bit, which comes in contact with the rock. The drill bit has holes that connect to the inner tube of the rod.

When the rig is vertically inserted into the ground, the high-pressure air travels through the outer tube downward to power the drill bit. The broken rock travels upward through the inner tube and is collected on the surface for sample examination.

One benefit of using RC drilling versus RAB drilling is that the rock samples from RC drilling contain no contamination from surrounding rocks because they travel cleanly to the surface. RAB drilling samples can easily come in contact with surrounding rock, giving inaccurate sample readings.

Watch the following YouTube video about RC drilling.

Atlas Copco RC50 Animation

www.goldminingbook.com/rcdrilling

Diamond Drilling

Diamond drilling is the most expensive and penetrative type of drilling. It can cost between $75 and $200 per meter and can penetrate as deep as 1,800 meters. Also, unlike other drilling methods, it recovers core samples of rock, not just rock chips.

This drilling method is called diamond drilling because it uses diamond-impregnated drill bits attached to the drill rods to cut a cylindrical core of solid rock. The diamonds are industrial grade diamonds and the ratio of diamonds to metal affect the performance of the bits' cutting ability.

Once drilled, the core samples are retrieved to the surface with a core tube. Then, the core is washed and broken into smaller pieces to fit into the sample trays. Half of the core samples are assayed while the other half are stored for future use. When the property changes hands, these samples will be passed on to the next owner. The stored samples may be re-assayed.

Fire Assay – Sample Testing

The goal of exploration drilling is to obtain rock samples that reveal information about the deposit underneath the surface. To make company-to-company comparisons possible, rock samples must be tested and analyzed according to strict guidelines.

Fire assaying is the most reliable quantitative testing method for accurately determining the amount of gold contained within a particular drill sample. For example, fire assaying tells the mining company whether there is 0.6 or 5 grams per tonne present inside a sample.

In gold mining, the grade is extremely important because it is one of the variables in the cost of production per ounce. If it costs $100 to mine and process one tonne of ore, there needs to be a high enough gold concentration within that tonne to make the extraction profitable.

For example, would it make sense to produce a deposit that contains 2 grams per tonne if the mining and processing costs are $100 per tonne? Let's check it out.

For every $100 that is spent, we get 2 grams of gold. To get one ounce of gold, we would need to process 15.5 tonnes because 1 troy ounce is equal to 31 grams. So, we would need to spend $1,550 to produce one ounce of gold. When the price of gold is less than $1,550 per ounce, it does not make any sense to produce from such a deposit. Note that I am keeping it simple. There are other costs such as exploration that need to be taken into account, but if the mining and processing costs alone are already higher than the price of gold, then the economic picture gets worse when other costs are included.

Let's do the same calculation for a gold deposit with grade of 5 grams per tonne.

In this situation, we would only need to process about 6.2 tonnes to get one ounce of gold, and instead of spending $1,550 to get it, we would spend only $620. This kind of deposit would most likely be economical because there is enough margin between the sales price and the costs to make a profit.

You probably would like me to give you a rule of thumb for what grade is good and what grade is bad. I would be doing you a disservice if I did that because there are too many variables that need to be considered. For example, a grade of 0.70 grams per tonne for one deposit might be fantastic but 2 grams per tonne on another deposit might be terrible. It depends on whether the mine will be open pit or underground, or whether the gold deposit is fully oxidized or sulfide.

If you have no idea what I just said, don't worry. That's why you are reading this book.

Anyway, fire assaying is a chemical process that is used to separate gold from other elements contained in the drill sample in order to find out the exact gold content. When samples are collected, they are carefully marked based on the exact location that they came from. Then, the samples are sent out to third-party laboratories for testing. The companies cannot do their own testing for the same reasons property owners cannot appraise their own properties.

When the results return, the companies report them to the investing public through press releases. This is when the stock prices can experience wild fluctuations based on what is reported and how it is perceived by investors. With that being said, do not assume that just because the drilling results are great that the stock price will automatically soar. It really depends on the market.

For example, during bear markets, like the one that we are in as I am writing this book, drilling results mean very little. Investors hate the mining companies so much that they do not even pay attention to the drilling results or any kind of news releases for that matter. Actually, good news sometimes causes stock prices to decrease because it gives sellers liquidity to get out.

The assay results of individual holes are also mapped out carefully to help geologists learn about the deposit and pinpoint future drilling.

Reading Drill Results

Since we are on the topic of assaying and drilling results, it would not be a bad idea to talk about reading drilling results. I cannot tell you how many times I received e-mails from gold mining investors asking me about drilling results because they do not know how to read them.

Let me be clear. Reading drill results is the easy part. It is interpreting them that is hard. In this section, I will only teach you how to read them, and hopefully when you are done, you will understand why I cannot possibly teach you how to interpret them. This is the job of a geologist.

Let's step back for a second. What are we trying to accomplish through drilling? We are trying to uncover a picture that is hidden underneath. Here is what I mean.

Let's assume that we are looking for the following picture.

The problem is that it is hidden somewhere and we don't know where. So, we look at a variety of geological maps and run geophysical and geochemical tests to help us find it. After we map out our findings, this is what we get.

Then, we sit down at the table with the other executives of our company and say, "We might have something here. This might be what we are looking for. Let's do some drilling to find out."

After drilling our first hole, we gain a little bit of visibility.

As you can see, we made a strike meaning that this hole was successful. We think that it might have something but we need to drill more to be sure.

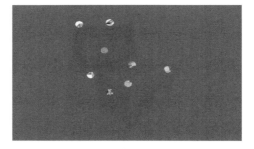

After drilling more successful holes, we realize that we getting a clearer picture of what is hidden underneath but we are not sure whether this is what we are looking for. Let's drill some more.

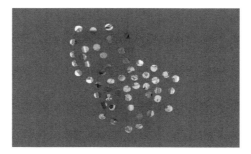

After drilling even more holes which are spaced closer to each other, we finally get to the point where we are sure that we found the picture/treasure that we were looking for. Now, we can move on to the next step, which is determining if we can extract it profitably.

This is all the exploration drilling is supposed to do – show you a picture of a gold deposit, assuming that there is one in the first place. The difference is that with a gold deposit, a mining company is trying to get a three-dimensional picture of it.

The only way to achieve this is to drill enough holes, analyze the samples, and map the results in a three-dimensional manner. There are software programs that do all that.

The results from individual holes tell geologists the three most important pieces of information:

- Where the ore body starts
- Where the ore body ends
- How much gold is in between the start and end

Drill Hole

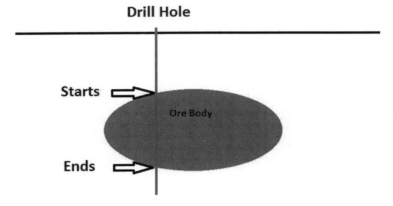

As you can see, the ore body starts X number of meters from the surface and it continues for Y number of meters until it ends. Then, the assaying tells the geologist what level of gold concentration was found between the starting and ending points.

So, when you read the individual drill results, this is all that you get.

For example, the following are assay results from RC drilling for Mary LC Deposit, which is owned by Scorpio Gold Corporation.

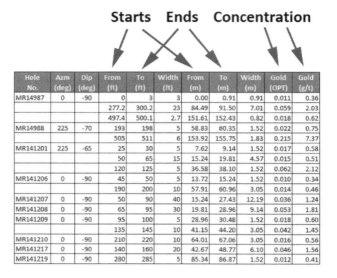

Starts   Ends   Concentration

Hole No.	Azm (deg)	Dip (deg)	From (ft)	To (ft)	Width (ft)	From (m)	To (m)	Width (m)	Gold (OPT)	Gold (g/t)
MR14987	0	-90	0	3	3	0.00	0.91	0.91	0.011	0.36
			277.2	300.2	23	84.49	91.50	7.01	0.059	2.03
			497.4	500.1	2.7	151.61	152.43	0.82	0.018	0.62
MR14988	225	-70	193	198	5	58.83	60.35	1.52	0.022	0.75
			505	511	6	153.92	155.75	1.83	0.215	7.37
MR141201	225	-65	25	30	5	7.62	9.14	1.52	0.017	0.58
			50	65	15	15.24	19.81	4.57	0.015	0.51
			120	125	5	36.58	38.10	1.52	0.062	2.12
MR141206	0	-90	45	50	5	13.72	15.24	1.52	0.010	0.34
			190	200	10	57.91	60.96	3.05	0.014	0.46
MR141207	0	-90	50	90	40	15.24	27.43	12.19	0.036	1.24
MR141208	0	-90	65	95	30	19.81	28.96	9.14	0.053	1.81
MR141209	0	-90	95	100	5	28.96	30.48	1.52	0.018	0.60
			135	145	10	41.15	44.20	3.05	0.042	1.45
MR141210	0	-90	210	220	10	64.01	67.06	3.05	0.016	0.56
MR141217	0	-90	140	160	20	42.67	48.77	6.10	0.046	1.56
MR141219	0	-90	280	285	5	85.34	86.87	1.52	0.012	0.41

As you can see, the table lists results for several holes, which in this example, are numbered starting with letters MR. Then, each hole's result shows where the gold deposit starts and ends both in feet and in meters. The gold concentration is listed in OPT (ounces per tonne) and g/t (grams per tonne). It also shows the angle of the drill hole which is important for a three-dimensional drawing.

Hopefully, now you are not going to be scared of looking at drilling results. In the future, if you get confused, always go back to the basics. What are they trying to accomplish? Then, think of the picture of the hidden treasure that I showed you. It is that simple.

DEPOSIT CLASSIFICATION

After enough holes are drilled in the ground and enough samples are analyzed in the lab, the mining company can finally estimate the size and grade of the deposit. At this point, the management might have an idea of whether the deposit is economical, and therefore will become a mine, but without further studies, they do not know for sure. In simple terms, all they know is that there is so much in the ground at X grade. Further studies are needed to figure out the best way to dig it out so that profitability can be achieved. Preliminary economic assessment (PEA), pre-feasibility and finally feasability studies are usually done with each one at a higher level of economic confidence. Usually a feasibility study is bankable meaning that you can borrow money on the economics of the project. The process of mining will be the focus of the next chapter.

In the gold mining industry, you might be asked, "How much gold does this company have in its NI 43-101?"

Before we get to the actual classification, let me talk about the 43-101. I like to think of the 43-101, or more specifically, the NI 43-101, as an appraisal report for a deposit. However, this report does not tell you the actual monetary value of the deposit.

The NI 43-101 is a very detailed report that describes the property, shows exploration drilling data, discusses assay procedures, reports resource and reserve estimates, and includes economic analysis. It is a standardized way of reporting and displaying information about mineral properties. It is written by an independent third-party engineering firm.

This standard was developed after the Bre-X Minerals Ltd. scandal in the 1990s during which a mining company defrauded investors by manipulating drilling samples (adding gold into them) to make their deposit appear extremely valuable. Because the investment community bought into the fraud, the stock price soared and the company's market cap reached $6.4 billion. Then, of course, when the fraud was exposed, the stock price collapsed, hurting a lot of investors in the process.

To protect investors from unscrupulous companies, new rules were developed, and now, if mining companies want to trade on certain exchanges and be taken seriously by investors, they have to follow these strict guidelines. Some people argue that these guidelines hurt investors more than help them because companies can barely say anything in their communications without a team of lawyers approving every word in their press releases. I have heard mining CEOs complain about how difficult it is for them to effectively communicate with shareholders because of the strict communication guidelines. Anyway, let's go back to discussing deposit classification.

Note that when I described the NI 43-101 report, one of the things that I said was that it "reports resource and reserve estimates." The following two tables are from an NI 43-101 Technical Report for Selinsing Gold Mine and Buffalo Reef Project Expansion, which are owned by Monument Mining.

Statement of Mineral Reserves

Area	Cutoff Grade	Proven			Probable			Proven + Probable		
	g/t	kt	g/t	koz	kt	g/t	koz	kt	g/t	koz
Oxide Reserves										
Selinsing	0.30	0	0.0	0.0	6	0.6	0.1	6	0.6	0.1
Buffalo Reef South & Central	0.30	14	1.6	0.7	336	19.0	20.8	350	1.9	21.5
Buffalo Reef North	0.31	12	0.9	0.3	155	1.2	5.7	166	1.1	6.1
Stockpile	0.30	2,335	0.7	53.6	0	0.0	0.0	2,335	0.7	53.6
Oxide Total		2,360	0.7	54.6	496	1.7	26.7	2,857	0.9	81.3
Sulfide Reserves										
Selinsing	0.62	183	2.7	16.1	630	2.2	44.6	812	2.3	60.7
Buffalo Reef South & Central	0.65	59	2.3	4.3	1,008	2.1	69.5	1068	2.2	73.8
Buffalo Reef North	0.66	4	1.5	0.2	130	1.5	6.1	133	1.5	6.3
Stockpile	0.62	20	1.3	0.8	0	0.0	0.0	20	1.3	0.8
Sulfide Total		266	2.5	21.4	1,768	2.1	120.2	2,034	2.2	141.7
Grand Total		2,626	0.9	76.0	2,264	2.0	146.9	4,890	1.4	222.9

Statement of Mineral Resources including Reserves

Area	Cutoff Grade	Measured			Indicated			Measured + Indicated			Inferred		
	g/t	kt	g/t	koz	kt	g/t	koz	kt	g/t	koz	kt	g/t	koz
Oxide Reserves													
Selinsing	0.27				9	0.7	0.2	9	0.7	0.2	3	0.6	0.1
Buffalo Reef South & Central	0.28	14	1.6	0.7	373	1.8	21.9	386	1.8	22.6	216	1.2	8.5
Buffalo Reef North	0.28	12	0.8	0.3	207	1.1	7.4	219	1.1	7.7	49	0.9	1.4
Stockpile	0.27	2,335	0.7	53.6				2,335	0.7	53.6			
Oxide Total		2,361	0.7	54.6	588	1.6	29.5	2,949	0.9	84.1	268	1.2	10.0
Sulfide Reserves													
Selinsing	0.56	229	2.2	16.0	1,436	1.9	88.4	1,664	2.0	104.5	121	1.1	4.5
Buffalo Reef South & Central	0.59	60	2.3	4.3	1,283	2.0	81.6	1,343	2.0	86.0	632	1.6	31.9
Buffalo Reef North	0.60	13	1.3	0.6	317	1.3	13.5	331	1.3	14.0	48	1.1	1.7
Stockpile	0.56	20	1.3	0.8				20	1.3	0.8			
Sulfide Total		322	2.1	21.7	3,036	1.9	183.6	3,358	1.9	205.3	801	1.5	38.0
Grand Total		2,682	0.9	76.3	3,624	1.8	213.0	6,307	1.4	189.4	1,070	1.4	48.0

I know that this is extremely confusing if you are new to gold mining, but bear with me.

The first thing I want you to pay attention to are the titles of the tables. The first table states, "Statement of Mineral Reserves," while the second table says, "Statement of Mineral Resources including Reserves."

To me, as a non-native English speaker, reserves and resources read and sound almost identical, so I really have to pay attention when someone says one versus the other.

By now, you should already know that just because there is a gold deposit in the ground does not mean that the gold can be extracted profitably. Also, part of the deposit might profitable while another part might not be. Also, a third part might be in a gray area where it could be profitable, but no one knows yet.

All of these probabilities of profitability have names. It starts with the term mineral resource.

A mineral resource has reasonable prospects for economic extraction. Resource is further divided into measured, indicated, and inferred.

Measured and indicated represent the part of the resource where enough drilling (more narrowly spaced drilling) has been done to show that the size and quality of the deposit is good enough to take it to the next level – a feasibility study. In other words, there is enough gold at a decent grade for us to move on and study whether we can extract it at a profit.

Inferred is like measured and indicated but not enough drilling has been done in the area to determine if it is worth moving on to the feasibility study. In other words, it is the remainder of the resource.

Because the measured and indicated parts of mineral resource show economic potential, the next set of studies proceeds. As I already mentioned, the study to figure out whether the mineral resource can be mined profitably is called a feasibility study. When measured and indicated ounces pass this test, they become reserves.

Another way of saying it is, reserve resource is a mineable (meaning economic) part of measured and indicated demonstrated by at least a preliminary feasibility study.

Reserve is further divided into proven and probable.

Proven mineral reserve is the economically mineable part of a measured mineral resource demonstrated by at least a preliminary feasibility study.

Probable mineral reserve is the economically mineable part of an indicated and, in some cases, a measured mineral resource demonstrated by at least a preliminary feasibility study.

In summary, there are two main mineral classifications which have subcategories.

Resource
- Measured and Indicated (second drilling program with more narrowly spaced holes)
- Inferred (first drilling program)

Reserve
- Proven (after feasibility study proves measured economic)
- Probable (after feasibility study proves measured and indicated economic)

CUT-OFF GRADE

If you go back to the reserve and resource table from the NI 43-101, you will also notice another column called the cut-off grade. This is the minimum grade that the ore must be in order for it to be profitably extracted. Any ore with a grade below the cut-off grade cannot be profitably produced. Consequently, any ore containing less than the cut-off grade is not included in the resource calculation. The cut-off grade is calculated during the feasibility study.

Because the NI 43-101 report is written for a particular set of data, the movement in the price of gold has effects on both the amount of resources and reserves and the cut-off grade. It makes sense because if the cut-off grade changes based on the price of gold, then the amount of resources and reserves also has to change.

[2]

Mining

[2]

Mining

IN THE PREVIOUS CHAPTER, you learned what mining companies have to do to find gold in the ground. This chapter is about getting it out of the ground and bringing it up to the surface.

Before getting into the details of how this is done, it would be helpful to define exactly what it is that they are trying to extract. You might say, gold, of course. Not so fast. It is the ore that they are trying to dig out.

Many people confuse ore and waste rock. Ore is rock that contains gold that is profitable to extract and waste rock is rock that does not. In an ideal world, you want to extract only ore and nothing else. Unfortunately, in order to get to the ore, you also have to extract some waste rock in the process. Some mining methods produce less waste rock than others.

I hope that now you can see why knowing just the grade of the deposit is not enough. You have to put it in the context of the entire mining process. What good is a high-grade deposit if you have to spend a fortune removing the waste rock to get to it?

With that being said, there are two ways to extract the ore – from the surface or underground. If the deposit is located close to the surface, you dig a big hole to get the ore. In other words, you build an open pit mine. However, if the deposit is located deep inside the Earth, then you cannot reach it from the surface. Well, you could, but it would not make economic sense. Can you imagine how much waste rock would have to be removed to get to it? Instead, it is more economical to go underground, so you build an underground mine.

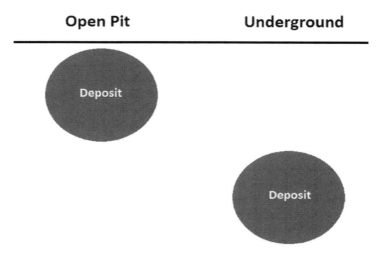

Let me ask you a question. If you had two identical deposits and the only difference was that one was close to the surface and the other one was deep inside the Earth, which one would be easier (also meaning cheaper) to access?

Of course, the deposit closest to the surface would be easier to access than the deeper deposit. Digging a hole is easier than building tunnels with proper ventilation, supports, and emergency exits.

Because of this simple fact, underground deposits need to have a higher gold concentration (higher grade) than open pit deposits in order to be economical. This is why an open pit deposit with a grade of 0.6 grams per tonne can be more desirable than an underground deposit with 2 grams per tonne.

OPEN PIT MINING

This is what an open pit mine looks like.

As you can see, an open pit mine looks like a big cone. The reason why open pit mines are shaped this way is because the ore and waste rock are removed in successive layers, which are called benches.

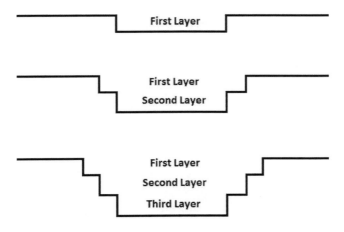

The mining process starts with the first layer or bench of material removed. Then, when the second bench of material is removed, the first bench is expanded in order to progress deeper and deeper into the ground. When the third bench is removed, both the second and first benches are expanded again. This process continues until the gold deposit has been depleted or the production becomes uneconomical. (When production from an open pit mine becomes uneconomical, the mining company might build an underground mine underneath the open pit mine).

Each layer is removed by blasting the rock with explosives, and using the excavator to place it into the huge haul trucks. The explosive material is inserted into very shallow drill holes. Remember how I told you that there is a difference between exploration drilling and production drilling? Well, here we are talking about production drilling.

One of the factors that determines the height of the bench is the reach of the excavator. Other factors include deposit geology, production strategy, and slope stability.

You might wonder, how do the dump trucks get the ore and waste rock to the top? The haul roads are built into the open pit mines as shown in the following illustration.

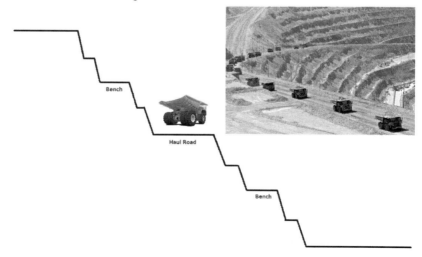

As you can see, it can be quite an interesting scene with one truck after another hauling the ore and waste. Because the transportation costs are high in relation to the entire cost of production, the waste material is dumped outside of the mined-out area in order to minimize the transportation costs.

Obviously, as open pit mines become deeper, the transportation costs increase. Sometimes mining companies construct long-distance conveyor systems to improve transportation costs (large upfront investment).

Now that you know the shape of open pit mines, what would be the perfect shape for a gold deposit? It would have to be the shape of a cone pointing downward.

The reason why a cone-shaped deposit would be a perfect deposit is because it would perfectly match an open pit mine. This means that there would be no waste rock being excavated and transported by dump trucks. Everything would be ore.

However, there is no such thing as the perfect deposit, and therefore, there is always waste rock that has to be extracted along with the ore.

The relationship between ore and rock waste is called the strip ratio.

Strip Ratio = Rock Waste Removed/Ore Removed

For a perfect deposit, the strip ratio would be zero since the nominator would be zero. Since we live in the real world, this would never happen outside of textbooks.

Obviously, the smaller the strip ratio the better. A strip ratio of one would mean that the company had to move one tonne of waste rock to extract one tonne of ore. A strip ratio of three would mean that the company had to move three tonnes of waste rock to extract one tonne of ore.

One other thing that is important to recognize is that the strip ratio changes throughout production. This is understandable because during the removal of each layer or bench, the relationship between the ore and waste rock changes depending on the shape of the deposit. Consequently, the cost of production also has to change during the life of mine (LOM). So, you might have an open pit mine that is extremely profitable at the beginning (low strip ratio) and less profitable at the end (high strip ratio).

Consequently, the mining companies might report a project's strip ratio for a certain period of time such as the first three years or they might report it for the entire life of mine which would be the average strip ratio.

You may want to know what is a good strip ratio. Again, this is also difficult to answer because there are other factors that come into play. What is the grade? If the grade is higher, then a higher strip ratio can be tolerated. How far is the processing facility? If it is far, then the strip ratio might have to be low to allow for profitability.

Everybody likes rules of thumb, but they are impossible in mining. There are not two identical mines. The best thing to do is to know the entire gold production process and understand how various factors affect each other. At the end of the day, what matters is whether the entire production can be profitable.

Open pit mining is generally for low-grade deposits that are located near the surface. All the high-grade deposits were already mined out years ago. Because open pit mining is used for low-grade deposits, a mining rate of more than 20,000 tonnes per day is usually necessary. Some open pits operate at a rate of 100,000 tonnes per day.

To put things in perspective, a 20,000-tonne-per-day mining production would require 100 trips by a 200-tonne haul truck. A 100,000-tonnes-per-day operation would require 500 of those trips. This is why you can find so many haul trucks at the same time to support a large mining operation. The carrying capacity of haul trucks ranges between 100 and 400 tonnes. These trucks are so big that they have to be shipped in pieces and assembled on site.

In summary, open pit mines are designed in a way to extract the ore from deposits that are located near the surface. The ore, along with the waste rock, is carried by the haul trucks. Some haul trucks carry the waste, which is dumped near the open pit mine. Other haul trucks carry the ore which is taken to the processing facility (usually straight to the primary crusher).

The processing of ore is discussed in the next chapter, but before we move on to processing, let's discuss underground mining.

UNDERGROUND MINING

When we think of mining in general, probably the first thing that comes to mind is dark tunnels, railroad tracks, and a flashlight on a miner's forehead. This is underground mining.

Unlike open pit mining, underground mining is generally for high-grade, deep ore bodies. Low-grade deposits are simply not economical. It costs too much money to access and extract ore located deep inside the Earth. Low-grade deposits do not generate enough revenues to cover the production and development costs of underground mining. However, if the price of gold were to increase to $3,000 or $5,000 per ounce, then low-grade ore bodies might become economical for underground mining.

Also, the mining rate of underground mines is much lower than the mining rate for open pit mines. If you recall from the previous section, open pit mines operate at a mining rate of more than 20,000 tonnes per day. Some produce as much as 100,000 tonnes per day. Open pit mining is bulk extraction. Underground mines, on the other hand, operate at mining rates of less than 20,000 tonnes per day. Actually, an underground mine with a mining rate of 10,000 tonnes per day is considered large. Consequently, mining companies are more selective when deciding whether to build an underground mine. Also, underground mining generates very little waste rock in relation to the ore so the strip ratio is not an important metric. In other words, underground mining generates little dilution.

Access

Because underground deposits are located deep inside the Earth, they obviously have to be accessed first before any extraction can take place. The access can be created through adits (horizontal mine entrances), mine shafts, vertical or horizontal tunnels, or declines (ramps, or gently sloping tunnels).

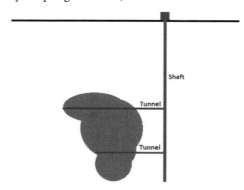

The graphic represents a simplified version of deposit access through a shaft and tunnels. However, real underground mines have complicated networks of tunnels and passes which are used for transporting equipment, people, and ore. Each mine has at least two shafts to provide ventilation and an alternative exit in case of emergency. In the old days, miners would send a canary to check whether it was safe to access the mine. Today, proper ventilation is required.

MINING METHODS

All open pit deposits are mined pretty much the same way – bulk extraction. However, because underground mining needs to produce very little waste rock, selective mining methods are used. There are several different mining methods used to extract ore from underground mines, and they are determined by the type of ore, the composition of the surrounding rock, and the shape and location of the ore deposit.

The ore in the underground mines is extracted through stoping. A stope is a large underground room that was created by removing ore. Imagine a deposit from which you cut out a horizontal rectangle as shown below. The following method is called cut-and-fill.

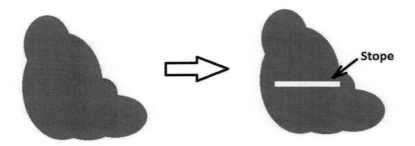

The rock that is removed from the deposit, thereby creating the stope, is the rock that contains mineralization. Through the tunnels and shafts, the ore is transported to the surface.

Depending on the hardness of the rock, the stope might need to be filled with cement, sand, waste rock, or other material to prevent caving.

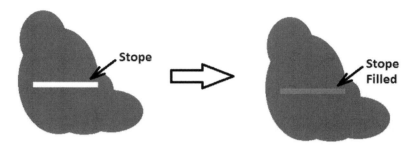

After the stope has been filled with supporting material, another stope can be created on top of the filled stope by extracting more ore.

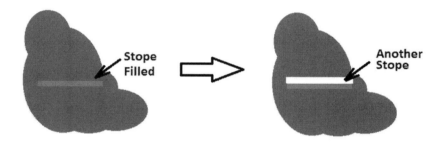

This process continues until all the ore has been fully extracted.

There are several underground mining methods which are categorized on the basis of the extent of support required: unsupported, supported, and caving.

Unsupported means that the rock is strong enough to support itself after the ore is extracted, and there is no backfill necessary. Obviously, unsupported mining methods are the most economical. You simply cut out the ore you want and leave. No cleanup necessary. Supported mining methods require backfill or other supporting techniques. They are expensive and used only if unsupported or caving methods are not suitable. Caving mining methods, as the name implies, allow the rock to collapse after the stopes are created and the ore is removed. The collapse is controlled instead of random.

Unsupported Mining Methods

The unsupported mining methods include room-and-pillar mining and sublevel stoping.

Room-and-Pillar Mining

Room-and-Pillar is one of the oldest mining methods. The ore is extracted across horizontal planes creating big rooms which are supported by pillars.

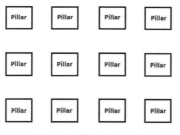

Bird's Eye View of the Underground Mine

The height of the room is tall enough to allow jumbo drills and haul trucks to maneuver, expanding the area. First, the jumbo drill vehicles make holes horizontally into the unpenetrated walls. Then, the explosives are inserted into the holes to break the ore into pieces. Finally, the haul trucks remove the ore.

If you have a hard time visualizing what I am describing, think of a big industrial room whose ceiling is supported by thick posts. In mining rooms, the ceiling is supported by posts called pillars.

For an even better illustration, watch the following YouTube video.

Room and Pillar Mining

www.goldminingbook.com/roomandpillar

The shape of the pillars can be rectangular or oval and the distance between them can vary. If possible, the mine engineers plan for the pillars to be located in low-grade areas of deposits. Also, on the first run, the pillars might be thicker to provide firm ceiling support, but during later runs, the pillars might be reduced in size to avoid leaving valuable ore behind. However, some ore must be left behind. This ore is not included in the NI 43-101 deposit estimates – it is the cost of doing business. The room-and-pillar method is best for relatively flat-lying deposits.

Sublevel Stoping

Another unsupported mining method is sublevel stoping. In this method, the access to the ore body is created at the bottom. Holes are drilled upward. When the ore body is fractured (in vertical stopes) by the explosive material, the ore falls down with gravity. The fractured ore is picked up at the bottom by a haul truck.

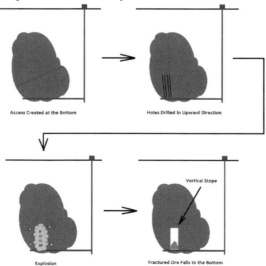

After the vertical stope has been cleared of fractured ore, the same process starts on the next vertical stope.

While sublevel stoping is best used for narrow and steeply dipping ore bodies, it could also be used for regularly shaped ore bodies. If the rock is very hard, then no backfill is necessary. However, if the rock is softer, then backfill might be necessary. In other words, sublevel stoping could be categorized as a supported or unsupported mining method.

For greater clarification, watch this sublevel stoping video.

Sublevel Stoping

www.goldminingbook.com/sublevelstoping

SUPPORTED MINING METHODS

The most popular supported mining method is cut-and-fill stoping, which I already discussed at the beginning of this section. It consists of removing horizontal slices (stopes) and filling them with cement or other supporting material. The backfill supports the stope walls and provides a working platform for mining equipment used in cutting the next stope. Another horizontal stope is cut out on top of the backfill through drilling, blasting, and removing. The cut-and-fill stoping method is used for steeply dipping ore bodies in moderately hard rock. It is also used for irregularly shaped deposits.

Watch the following video on cut-and-fill stoping.

Cut and Fill Stoping

www.goldminingbook.com/cutandfillstoping

CAVING MINING METHODS

The caving mining methods include sublevel caving and block caving.

Sublevel Caving

In sublevel caving, the ore body is divided into horizontal layers. Similarly to sublevel stoping, holes are drilled in the ceiling in order to blast the ore. This time, not only the blasted ore falls down due to gravity but the surrounding ore caves in. Obviously, the rock cannot be very hard or it won't cave. With the sublevel caving method, the extraction work can take place on different sublevels at the same time. No backfill is applied.

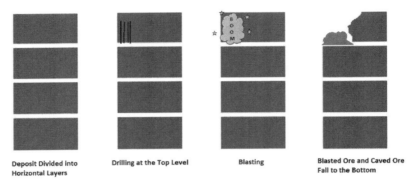

| Deposit Divided into Horizontal Layers | Drilling at the Top Level | Blasting | Blasted Ore and Caved Ore Fall to the Bottom |

The sublevel caving method is used for the extraction of vertical and massive deposits. Also, it is often carried out under the open pit deposit because at some point, open pit deposits become uneconomical due to the high strip ratio. Consequently, a transition to underground mining using sublevel caving might make the deposit economical again.

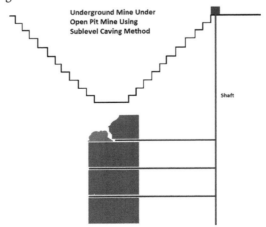

Underground Mine Under Open Pit Mine Using Sublevel Caving Method

Shaft

Sublevel Caving video.

www.goldminingbook.com/sublevelcaving

Block Caving

Block caving is another caving mining technique. Unlike other underground mining methods, block caving is a mass mining method. Because of its economies of scale, the operating costs are low. Consequently, it is used for large, relatively lower-grade ore deposits. While the operating costs are low, the development costs are high, so mining companies have to balance between the two. Similar to sublevel caving, block caving is often considered for mining ore bodies that are located or extend beneath open pit mines. A major problem when planning for block caving is predicting in advance whether the specific ore bodies will cave as originally hoped.

For me, the best way to explain the block caving method is to visualize a skyscraper being blow up from the bottom.

After the explosion destroys the support of the building, gravity causes the entire structure to collapse into the ground.

This is what block caving is all about. To carry out the block caving technique, a grid of tunnels is developed right under the large and, hopefully, vertical ore body. The explosive material is inserted into the drilled holes. The whole thing is blasted causing the ore body to fracture upward. Finally, the fractured ore is removed by haul trucks.

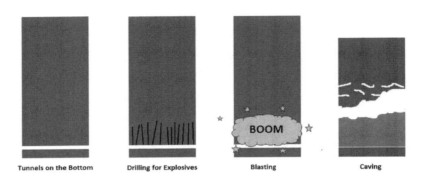

| Tunnels on the Bottom | Drilling for Explosives | Blasting | Caving |

When done properly, the block caving method delivers huge production at a small cost. However, if the ore body does not cave as predicted, this could cause financial stress on the company because once block caving has been established, there is no flexibility to alter the mining method.

Block Caving

www.goldminingbook.com/blockcaving

Narrow Vein Mining

So far, all the mining methods discussed dealt with continuous ore bodies. However, gold mineralization may also occur in narrow veins of less than one meter wide. The extraction of such ore requires different methods.

More than 100 years ago, narrow vein mining was predominant. However, as machinery was introduced, other mining methods became more effective. The problem with narrow vein deposits is that they are erratic and variable. Today's traditional mining methods would produce too much dilution, meaning that too much waste rock would be extracted with the ore.

Because of the erratic nature of narrow vein deposits, the extraction is less mechanized and more labor intensive (labor means expensive). Consequently, they are less desirable.

The following video is an example of Narrow Vein Mining.

MVM1100 Narrow Vein Mining

www.goldminingbook.com/narrowvein

Ore Transportation

The goal in choosing the right mining method is to extract the ore at the lowest cost possible with very little waste rock. Sometimes one method is appropriate, and other times, another method is better. Also, it is not unusual for a mining company to use different mining methods for the same ore body which could be shaped differently at various locations.

After the ore is removed from the stopes, it is moved through a carefully designed transportation system. In underground mining, ore transportation significantly affects profitability. First, the ore is dumped through tunnels and passes into a central location underground. Next, it is usually crushed in a big underground crusher that breaks it into smaller pieces. Finally, the crushed ore is transported to the surface via rail, shaft, conveyor belt, or load haul dump truck.

Once the ore reaches the surface, it is transported to a processing facility through conveyor belts or trucks. The processing of ore is the topic of the next chapter.

[3]

Processing

[3]

Processing

IN THE PREVIOUS TWO chapters, you learned how gold deposits are found and how they are mined out of the ground. However, at this point, there is no pure gold yet. All that has been done so far is the extraction of ore and ore is not pure gold.

Ore is nothing but rock. Yes, it contains gold, but the gold particles are so small that most of the time, you cannot even see them. Consequently, the next step is to separate the gold from the ore. This requires processing, which is the topic of this chapter.

There are many types of ore. However, for our purposes, there are only two types of ore: easy-to-process and hard-to-process ore.

Easy-to-process ore is called free-milling ore. It is ore from which gold can be recovered using conventional recovery methods. Hard-to-process ore is rebellious ore and it is called refractory ore. If you just used conventional processing methods with refractory ore, you would get extremely low recoveries making the entire operation uneconomical. Therefore, refractory ore requires pretreatment before it can undergo traditional recovery methods. Because it requires additional work, the processing costs more.

Conventional Recovery Process

Let's start with the conventional recovery process for easy-to-process or free-milling ore.

Crushing

When the ore arrives at the processing facility, it is in the form of broken rock. If the ore came from an underground mine, it may have already been crushed underground by a big crusher before reaching the surface. However, if the ore came from an open pit mine, then it will not have been crushed yet.

So, the first step in processing is to crush the ore into a smaller size. Generally, the finer the crushing, the better the recoveries. Sometimes, mining companies choose not to crush at all (mostly open pit ore) because the blasting fractured the rock finely enough to obtain respectable recoveries. In this case, the ore is called run-of-mine ore. At other times, the ore is crushed several times by multiple crushers. The crush size depends on the recovery method used.

Gravity Separation

After crushing, the ore can go directly through heap leaching (next section) which is the most popular recovery technique, or it can first go through gravity separation.

The gravity separation recovery method has been around for thousands of years. It is the cheapest in terms of capital and operational costs. It is also the most environmentally friendly technique.

Remember how I told you at the beginning of the book that gold has a specific gravity of 19.3? Well, gravity separation uses the force of gravity to separate it from the rest of the ore. Gold ore has a specific gravity of between 2 and 3.

The simplest gravity separation technique is gold panning.

The prospector combines water with the crushed ore. When shook, the water makes the heavy gold fall to the bottom while leaving the dirt on top. Of course, during gold production, you could have hundreds of prospectors panning to separate the gold from the ore, but this would be prohibitively expensive. The price of gold would have to be much higher to justify these labor costs.

Today, gold mining companies use large gravity separation machines that accomplish the same thing on a larger scale. The machines use water and a shaking table to separate gold from the ore. Another type of device used is a Knelson concentrator, which spins and creates a centifugal force. This concentrates the heavy particles, which inlude gold.

While gravity separation has its advantages, it also falls short. The problem is that gravity separation recovers very little gold. The recoveries can be between 0 and 50 percent. The method works very well when gold is in its free elemental state, which is rare in today's gold deposits. Consequently, the gravity separation technique is used as a supplemental method incorporated into the entire recovery process.

CYANIDATION

As mentioned before, gravity separation is environmentally friendly. This is because it uses no chemicals. Another process, cyanidation is all about chemicals, so it is anything but environmentally friendly. Despite the unfriendliness to the environment, cyanidation is responsible for the majority of gold extraction today.

Cyanidation is a method of using cyanide to extract gold from the ore. Cyanide is a chemical compound that can be found in low concentrations in fruits, nuts, plants, and insects. It can also be created by humans in a lab. When cyanide comes in contact with gold, something interesting happens. Gold dissolves in cyanide the same way sugar dissolves in hot water. In other words, gold that you can touch turns into liquid.

Therefore, what mining companies do is crush the ore as previously discussed and mix it with cyanide. Cyanide trickles through the ore sucking the gold away from it. Brilliant, isn't it? Chemistry is a wonderful thing. The process of dissolving gold away from the ore is called leaching and it can take as little as 24 hours and as long as 90 days or more. It all depends on the leaching methods which are discussed later.

After the leaching process, there are two substances left: liquid and dirt. The liquid is the cyanide with dissolved gold and the dirt is the crushed rock with no more gold. Actually, it still contains some gold because no technique has a 100 percent recovery rate. The dirt that has been stripped of gold is called tailings. By regulation, tailings have to be discarded and managed according to specific procedures.

The liquid portion is called a pregnant solution. During the leaching process, the pregnant solution is collected.

The next step is to separate the gold from the rest of the solution. There are two main processes to accomplish this: carbon loading and the Merrill-Crowe zinc precipitation process.

During the carbon loading process, the pregnant solution comes in contact with activated carbon. Gold is adsorbed by or gets stuck onto the surface of the activated carbon (created from coconut husks). Then, the gold has to be detached from the carbon through a process called carbon stripping. Some mining companies might do the carbon stripping in-house or they might ship the loaded carbon to a third-party processor. Carbon stripping is achieved through a process called elution, which results in a solution referred to as a pregnant eluate. The gold is removed from this solution by a process called electrowinning. After the gold is freed, it is back in solid form, ready for melting, pouring and refining.

The Merrill-Crowe (named after founders C.W. Merrill and T.B. Crowe) zinc precipitation process is an older method of separating gold from the pregnant solution. First, oxygen is removed from the liquid solution. When gold was originally being dissolved in cyanide, plenty of oxygen had to be supplied. The presence of oxygen helped gold turn into liquid. So, to turn gold back to solid form, oxygen had to be removed. Then, the pregnant solution was mixed with fine zinc powder. The zinc caused a chemical reaction with cyanide leaving the gold behind. The gold then precipitates or turns into solid form and is ready for melting, pouring and refining. In general, the Merrill-Crowe method requires more capital to construct and is operationally more expensive than activated carbon methods. Consequently, the ore has to be higher grade to justify additional expenditures. If the ore has a high silver content, the Merrill-Crowe method is preferred.

For better clarity, let me summarize the process in a picture illustration.

The process started with ore, which was turned into a liquid (pregnant solution) through leaching. Then, the liquid came in contact with carbon or zinc to be separated from the cyanide. If the pregnant solution was mixed with carbon, then additional steps (carbon stripping and electrowinning) were required to turn gold into solid form. If the pregnant solution was combined with zinc, then the process to arrive at solid gold was shorter. Either way, once gold was free, it was poured into what is called a doré bar.

Now that you understand the process, let's discuss various methods of leaching, carbon loading, and carbon stripping.

LEACHING

As you know, leaching is the process of mixing cyanide with ore in order for gold to dissolve in cyanide. Note that this only applies to oxide ore, not sulfide. There are two main methods for leaching: heap leaching and tank leaching. Because of the names, they should be easy to remember. In heap leaching, the leaching process takes place on heaps and in tank leaching, it happens in tanks.

Heap Leaching

The word heap is defined as a group of things placed on top of each other.

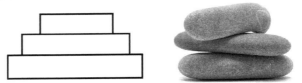

So, during heap leaching, the ore is stacked in heaps and sprinkled with cyanide from the top. The size of the heaps can range from a few acres to several hundred acres.

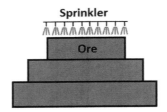

It takes between 60 and 90 days for the cyanide to percolate through the ore, dissolving the gold. The resulting pregnant solution is collected in a pond located next to the heap. In order to improve the drainage of the solution to the pond, the heap is constructed at an angle.

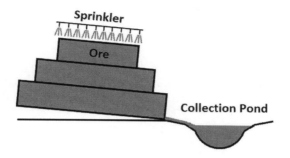

Heap leaching is attractive to mining companies due to the low capital and operational costs, the simplicity of the design, and the shorter start-up times. The operating costs can be less than $2 per tonne. However, the negatives are that heap leaching takes several months and yields recoveries between 50 and 80 percent. As with everything in mining, the costs and benefits have to be weighed to ensure profitability and a return on capital. Heap leaching is a very popular leaching method used mainly for low-grade, open pit deposits.

Tank Leaching

Heap leaching is used for lower-grade deposits where it is not worth spending the extra money to increase recoveries of the low-grade material. However, when the deposit in question is high-grade ore, then spending the extra money to increase the recoveries may be worth it. This is where tank leaching comes into play. The development requires more capital and it costs more operationally but the recoveries can be between 70 and 90 versus 50 and 80 percent for heap leaching. Also, the leaching process takes 24 hours versus 90 days or more.

For tank leaching, the ore is crushed and finely ground into the size of powder. This is different than for heap leaching which sometimes uses uncrushed ore (run-of-mine ore). For tank leaching, the ore has to be finer because it gets mixed with a reagent inside a tank to form a slurry or pulp. (Tank leaching is also called pulp leaching.) The slurry is created because slurry leaches faster – hence a 24-hour leaching process versus 90 days. The slurry is agitated with air injection to provide oxygen. As mentioned before, oxygen is needed to help gold turn into liquid. The air injection is not needed for heap leaching because heap leaching is done outside in the open air. Because of the agitation process, tank leaching is also called agitated tank leaching or agitated pulp leaching. Finally, the agitated slurry is mixed with cyanide, which is able to dissolve gold in a matter of hours. The result is a pregnant solution.

CARBON LOADING

After leaching, the pregnant solution is combined with activated carbon through one of two processes: carbon-in-pulp (CIP) and carbon-in-column (CIC).

Carbon-in-Pulp

In the carbon-in-pulp method, the activated carbon comes in contact with the pregnant solution inside the same tanks where tank leaching took place. In other words, carbon-in-pulp and tank leaching go hand in hand. The carbon is mixed with the cyanide leach solution by being applied straight to the slurry or pulp. So, it is added while the gold is still being dissolved in cyanide. Carbon-in-pulp is not used with heap leaching.

Carbon-in-Column

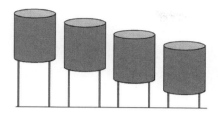

Every time you see tanks stacked from the highest to the lowest, you know that the company is using a carbon-in-column method, which is always used with heap leaching, unless, of course, the Merrill-Crowe zinc precipitation process is used.

After the heap leaching process, the pregnant solution is passed through a series of columns which all contain activated carbon. As you already know, the gold adsorbs onto the carbon. Then, the loaded carbon is periodically removed from the columns.

CARBON STRIPPING

There are several different methods for carbon stripping, such as Zadra stripping, the Anglo American Research Laboratory (AARL) stripping, and alcohol stripping. However, they all use elution to separate carbon from gold.

During elution, the loaded carbon is placed in a container with a hot solution that redissolves the gold, separating it from the surface of the carbon. An example of such a solution is (1%) sodium hydroxide and (0.1%) cyanide. Notice that I said "hot" solution. Temperature is very important. It helps gold peel away from carbon.

During the carbon loading, low temperatures were used because gold sticks to carbon at low temperatures. However, at high temperatures, gold peels away from carbon.

Upon the completion of elution, gold is back in liquid form inside a new solution called the pregnant eluate. To be set free, it has to go through electrowinning.

ELECTROWINNING

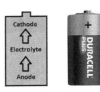

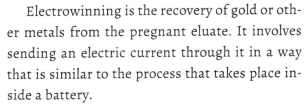

Electrowinning is the recovery of gold or other metals from the pregnant eluate. It involves sending an electric current through it in a way that is similar to the process that takes place inside a battery.

At the edges of a battery, there are two electrodes: a cathode on the top and an anode on the bottom. The electrolyte is in the middle. An electrolyte (pregnant eluate, in this case) is a fluid that allows the flow of electricity between the anode and the cathode.

During the gold recovery process, the anode and the cathode, which are made of steel or stainless steel, are placed inside the pregnant eluate.

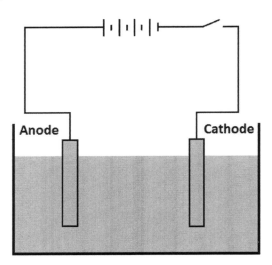

When the switch is flipped to the on position, the electric current starts flowing from the anode to the cathode in a counterclockwise direction.

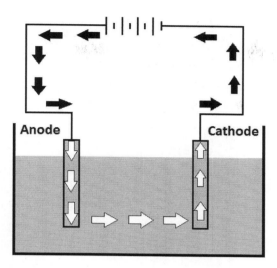

As the electricity goes through the pregnant eluate, gold goes through a chemical reaction. It is sucked out of the solution and deposits on top of the cathode in solid form.

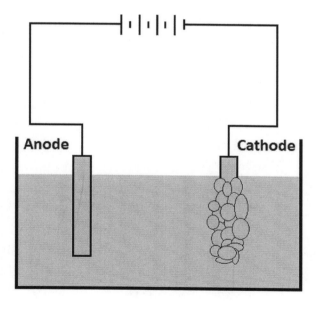

Then, the cathode (made of stainless steel), with gold, is placed into a melting furnace and heated to 2,000° F. At this temperature, gold melts but stainless steel does not because the melting point of stainless steel is 2,550° F, while the melting point of gold is 1,946° F.

The melted gold is poured into a doré bar.

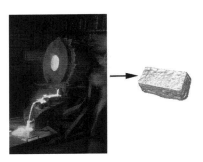

UNCONVENTIONAL RECOVERY PROCESS

Up to this point, everything that you have read about in this chapter was related to the recovery process for easy-to-process ore. There is another category of ore that that does not respond well to conventional recovery processes. I am talking about refractory ore.

To be refractory means to disobey or resist authority or control. In our case, the disobedience is toward cyanide. So, refractory ore does not respond well to cyanidation.

If you recall from the previous discussions, gold particles are released from ore when they come in contact with cyanide. With refractory ore, gold particles are not allowed to come in contact with cyanide. They are encapsulated or physically locked up inside other minerals that either stop cyanide from reaching gold or that consume cyanide themselves.

The main contributors to ore's refractoriness are sulfides and carbons. Pyrite, an iron sulfide, is the most common sulfide mineral. When cyanide is given a choice between gold or a sulfide mineral, it will always choose the sulfide mineral. Cyanide will combine with sulfide to form thiocyanate, which is an anion. You don't have to know what thiocyanate is or what it does. All you have to know is that when sulfide minerals are present, cyanide gets used up and there is very little or nothing left to dissolve gold.

Naturally occuring carbon is also problematic – it prevents proper leaching. After cyanide dissolves gold, carbon simply steals it away from the pregnant solution and the leaching process is back to square one. The stealing of gold has a name – preg-robbing. Note that during carbon loading, the same thing happens – carbon sucks out gold from the pregnant solution. However, at that point, it is not called robbing because this is what is wanted.

The refractory ore can contain sulfides or carbons and it can contain both at the same time. When it contains both, it is twice as rebellious, and therefore, is called double refractory.

The bottom line is this – sulfides and carbons are bad for recovering gold from ore. Somehow, these two substances have to be reduced or eliminated. In order for gold particles to be able to interact with cyanide, pretreatment is necessary. After pretreatment, gold particles can go through the conventional recovery process. As you can probably imagine, because extra steps are required, producing gold from refractory deposits is more expensive than producing it from regular deposits.

While there are many types of pretreatment methods, they all have one thing in common – the oxidation of the refractory material in order to eliminate it. The most common pretreatment methods include: roasting, autoclaving, bioleaching, and bacterial oxidation.

ROASTING

Roasting involves heating the ore in order to burn away the sulfur. At high temperatures, almost all sulfide minerals will oxidize (meaning combine with oxygen). When sulfur combines with oxygen, it is converted into sulfur dioxide, and like carbon dioxide from our cars, sulfur dioxide is a gas that is emitted to the atmosphere. By converting sulfur into sulfur dioxide, you get rid of the sulfur and the ore is no longer refractory. Consequently, the gold can be recovered with traditional recovery techniques, such as cyanide treatment.

Roasting also removes carbon which also oxidizes inside a roaster. When carbon combines with oxygen, it turns into carbon monoxide (dangerous) and carbon dioxide. Both of them are gases which are emitted to the atmosphere.

Because of all these gases, roasting is extremely unfriendly to the environment. As a result, in some countries, it is difficult or even impossible to get a permit for the construction of a roaster. However, companies are now using various gas-scrubbing systems to make roasting less environmentally destructive.

I used to own stock in Veris Gold which is located in Elko, Nevada. The company owns one of only three roasters in the state. Many investors invested in it because the government would not allow any new roasters to be built in the state, and this gave the existing owners a competitive advantage. Unfortunately, the price of gold has declined so dramatically over the last four years that the company still struggles with profitability. This is because production from refractory ore is expensive. A mining company with refractory ore cannot ever be the lowest-cost producer when other mining companies have non-refractory ore.

Building a roaster is capital intensive which means that it is only justifiable for large operations. Also, the energy consumption to run a roaster is very high.

AUTOCLAVING

Because roasting is extremely polluting to the environment, mining companies have had to develop alternative pretreatment methods. Autoclaving, also known as pressure oxidation, is one of those methods. The advantage of autoclaving over roasting is that it is much less pollutive and yields greater recoveries. The disadvantages include its inability to overcome carbon, and higher capital and operating costs (requires highly trained workers). So, autoclaving works with sulfide ore, but not with carbonaceous ore. Because of high capital costs, autoclaving, like roasting, is only suitable for large operations.

An autoclave is a container where pressure oxidation is conducted. It is essentially a pressure cooker. Inside the autoclave, sulfides are oxidized by pure oxygen under pressure – hence the name pressure oxidation. Also, this is done at high temperatures.

BIO-OXIDATION

Bio-oxidation is a process where the sulfide minerals are oxidized using bacteria. The oxidation takes place in tanks.

Unlike roasting and autoclaving, bio-oxidation has lower capital and operating costs making it suitable for smaller operations and for the pretreatment of lower-grade ore. Energy consumption is low. Start-up times are short. It is environmentally friendlier because there is no polluting sulfur dioxide emitted into the atmosphere.

The drawback of bio-oxidation is that the oxidation process is slow so it can yield low rates of production. The reason why the process is slow is because high temperatures cannot be used. As you remember from the previous sections, high temperatures speed up the oxidation process. However, if the temperature is too high, then the bacteria itself is killed.

Bio-oxidation also works to disarm carbon by oxidizing it and reducing its ability to steal away gold particles.

CHEMICAL OXIDATION

As I mentioned before, all the pretreatment methods are about oxidizing the refractory material. In chemical oxidation, chlorine, a strong oxidizing agent, is used to get the job done. Chlorine is a chemical element with the symbol Cl. Chemical oxidation is also called chlorination oxidation. This method successfully deactivates carbon. While chemical oxidation also eliminates sulfur, it is not very economical because sulfides consume exorbitant amounts of chlorine. The whole process takes place in tanks.

FLOTATION

By now, you should have it ingrained in your head that processing refractory ore is operationally expensive and building pretreatment facilities costs a lot of money. Because the profit margins on sulfide ore are razor thin, especially during low gold prices, companies do as much as they possibly can to improve efficiencies and lower production costs. One thing that they can do is use the flotation gold recovery method right before the pretreatment through roasting, autoclaving, bio-oxidation, or chemical oxidation. So, you can think of flotation as pretreatment before pretreatment.

Flotation is a separation method based on a mineral's ability to attach to air bubbles. This is especially useful for sulfide ore because sulfur and gold attach to air bubbles. Carbon also attaches to air bubbles. It is rare to use the flotation process on easy-to-treat ore.

If you can separate the valuable sulfide minerals from the worthless material before the expensive pretreatment process, then you have less ore to pretreat. This obviously lowers overall costs of production.

In the flotation process, very finely ground ore and water are mixed together in a tank.

A foaming agent is introduced to the mixture, too, to create a slurry. Then, when air is pumped into the mixture, air bubbles form. The sulfide and gold attach to the air bubbles and float with them to the top.

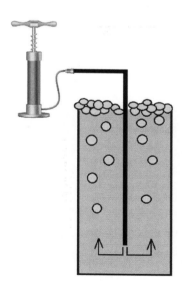

The resulting froth or foam containing the valuable material is collected. Gold is now in the form of a concentrate and is taken for the pretreatment process previously discussed.

BACK TO CONVENTIONAL RECOVERY METHODS

I know that I have thrown a lot of chemistry and complicated concepts at you. If you have a hard time understanding these processes, reread their descriptions again because if you are interested in gold mining companies, then you should know what they do to produce gold.

To summarize, there are two types of ore: easy-to-process and hard-to-process ore. The easy-to-process ore (for example, fully oxidized ore) is processed through conventional gold recovery methods. The hard-to-process ore does not allow gold particles to come in contact with cyanide in order to be dissolved. Consequently, it has to be pretreated. All the pretreating methods have one thing in common – oxidize, oxidize, and oxidize. Whether they use high temperatures, pressure, bacteria, or chemicals, in the end, they all combine oxygen with sulfur or carbon to make the ore easier to process. Before moving on to the next chapter, there is one more recovery method that can be used instead of cyanidation.

AMALGAMATION

Remember how gold particles dissolve in cyanide? Well, they also dissolve when combined with mercury. This is what the amalgamation method is about. Amalgamation is one of the oldest gold recovery methods.

The ore is finely crushed and treated with mercury. Mercury dissolves gold. The resulting solution or substance is called an amalgam. To free gold from the amalgam, the solution is heated and mercury evaporates into the atmosphere leaving gold behind. This is much simpler than going through leaching, carbon loading, and carbon stripping. However, the problem is that amalgamation is not favored by regulators and environmentalists.

With that being said, the amalgamation technique is still used today but it is definitely not as popular as cyanidation. In addition to being environmentally problematic, amalgamation yields low recovery rates (around 70 percent). Consequently, for large operations, this is not good enough. However, small operators looking for a quick way to process high-grade ore without trying to squeeze the last ounce of gold from it may find amalgamation suitable.

[4]
Refining

[4]

Refining

AT THIS POINT, I could stop the book because the role of the mining company and its employees is over. They found the gold. They mined it either through open pit or underground mining. They processed it, and then, they poured the gold into a doré bar.

You might look at this picture and say, "This is not what I thought the finished product looked like. It is not shiny or pretty the way I have seen on television."

Well, this is because mining companies do not refine gold into the finished product that we are accustomed to seeing. It is refining companies that do the refining. They take the rough-looking bar and turn into a beautiful, shiny, and pure bar of gold.

Refining companies are separate entities that have to be approved and accredited in order to be in the refining business. However, before refining a single bar of gold, they first have to purchase it.

Sale Transaction

After a mining company pours gold into a doré bar, it has a product to sell. However, this product cannot be sold on international exchanges yet, because it does not meet the gold purity requirements. A doré bar is an alloy of gold combined with other materials such as silver. Usually, the bar contains between 70 and 80 percent gold, 10 and 15 percent silver, and 5 and 20 percent other metal. The exchanges require the gold content to be between 99.50 and 99.99 percent.

Because the mining companies are not in the refining business, the doré bar is generally sold to a refining company that is capable of transforming it into a product that meets the requirements of the exchanges. As a prudent buyer, the refiner needs to examine the exact metal composition, which is important in determining the price that it will pay the miner. However, just by looking at it, no one can tell the exact metal composition. The miner already knows what it is, but the refiner cannot just blindly listen to the miner and pay for 80 percent gold content when, in reality, there is only 70 percent present.

To determine the exact content, the refiner melts down the doré bar and conducts its own assay. Upon completion, the refiner issues an outturn, which is an appraisal report indicating the weight of the doré bar and its exact composition in terms of gold, silver, and other metals.

As with any laboratory test, the results vary. In other words, the miner's results are slightly different from the refiner's results. Consequently, the two parties negotiate and settle on a price. The miner walks away with cash while the refiner takes ownership of the doré bar. This is when the refining process begins.

REFINING PROCESS

The job of the refiner is to add value and improve the product. It must buy the doré bar for a low enough price so that it can still make a profit after the refining costs are included. In this case, the refiner buys a gold bar that contains between 70 and 80 percent pure gold and must turn it into a new gold bar that contains 99.50 or 99.99 percent pure gold.

99.50 PERCENT

The refiners use a refining method called the Miller Process to achieve gold of 99.50 percent purity. As the name implies, the process was invented by Francis Bowyer Miller. It is also called the chlorine refining process because of the use of chlorine.

In the Miller process, the doré bar is melted in an induction furnace where chlorine gas is added to the molten substance creating chlorine bubbles. The unwanted or secondary metals such as silver and other metals react with chlorine and form liquid chlorides which float to the top. Then, they are removed, leaving 99.50 percent gold behind. Gold also likes to react with chlorine, but the other metals react with it faster, and they are separated from gold before gold forms its own reaction with chlorine.

At this point, the molten gold can be poured into a 99.50 percent gold bar. This is the minimum. A gold bar with a level of purity below 99.50 percent is not suitable for direct sale. It needs to be at least 99.50 percent gold in order to be used for industrial or investment purposes.

99.99 Percent

A high-content gold bar is a finished product after the long and arduous mining process. However, not all bars are the same. Some are bigger than others. Some are rounded. And, some contain more gold (99.99 percent) than others (99.50 percent). There are more than 50 types of gold bars.

The shape, weight, and concentration are dependent on which exchange the particular gold bar will trade. There are several gold exchanges around the world. Some are physical gold exchanges while others are commodity futures exchanges that allow physical deliveries.

The most important physical gold exchange is LBMA which stands for London Bullion Market Association. Refiners that supply gold to this exchange must meet specific guidelines. The gold bar must weigh between 350 and 430 ounces and contain a minimum purity of 99.50 percent gold. It must also have a serial number and seal representing the refiner. LBMA only accepts one type of bar while other exchanges accept more.

Some of the commodity futures exchanges are the COMEX, the Tokyo Commodity Exchange, and the Shanghai Gold Exchange.

For the COMEX, the gold bar must weigh 100 ounces (between 95 and 105 to be more specific) and have a minimum gold purity of 99.50 percent.

The COMEX also accepts 1,000-gram bars.

For the Shanghai Gold Exchange, the gold bar must weigh 3,000 grams and have a minimum purity of 99.95 percent, which is higher than the 99.50 percent required by the other two exchanges.

As you can see, a gold purity of 99.50 percent is acceptable by many of the exchanges. However, most investors prefer gold with 99.99 percent purity, so refiners have to deliver what the end customers want. To get from 99.50 to 99.99 percent, additional refining steps need to take place.

Gold has to go through the electrolytic refining process known as the Wohlwill process developed by Dr. Emil Wohlwill. The Wohlwill process uses an electric current to further refine gold. Remember how in the previous chapter, I briefly showed you the design of a battery?

The Wohlwill process also uses the design of a battery to refine gold. As you know, both the anode and the cathode have to be made of a material that conducts electricity. It could be silver, zinc, aluminum, or gold. In real life, we do not see too many electrodes made of gold because gold is so expensive that cheaper metals are used.

During the Wohlwill process, both the anode and the cathode are made of gold. However, there is a little difference though. The anode is made of the 99.50 percent pure gold that the refiner gets from the Miller process. The cathode is made of 99.99 percent pure gold that the refiner gets from an inventory of previously refined gold.

Both the anode and the cathode are placed in hydrochloric acid which serves as the electrolyte (fluid in the middle).

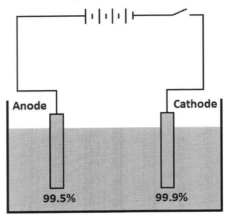

When the switch is turned on, the electricity starts to flow from the anode to the cathode in a counterclockwise fashion.

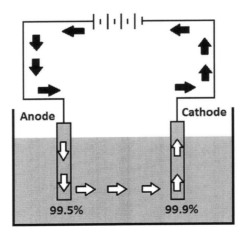

A chemical reaction takes place and something interesting happens. The gold from the anode dissolves while the silver and other metals do not. The dissolved gold travels to the cathode and gets deposited on top of it.

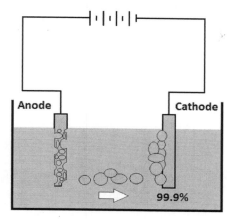

When the process is complete, the gold on the cathode is 99.99 percent pure gold. The job is done. The cathode is melted and poured into a beautiful gold bar that meets the specific requirements of an exchange.

Finally, the refining company sells the gold bar and the production process is finished.

[5]

Conclusion

[5]

Conclusion

FINALLY, WE ARRIVE AT the end. In this book, you learned what it takes to produce gold all the way from the beginning. You learned how mining companies find deposits, how they mine them, and how they process the ore. Also, you learned how the refiners take the rough-looking doré bars and turn them into objects of beauty.

While there is a lot of information covered in this short book, there is a lot that is not covered. For example, I did not address the permitting process or ownership rights and here is why.

I wanted to focus on the four basic stages that are universal. It does not matter whether a mine is in the US, Peru, or Chile; the process that I described is the same everywhere. However, if I included permitting, I would have had to discuss it for all the countries. This is a vast topic.

Hopefully, with the knowledge from this book, you will be able to look at various mining companies and understand what you have in front of your eyes. When you open an annual report and you read about gravity circuits, carbon stripping, and heap leaching, you will not run away. You will feel confident because you will finally have the tools to learn and analyze these companies better. This does not mean that you will automatically make money investing in them, especially when the entire industry is in a horrible bear market, but your chances will improve.

Suggested Reading

Suggested Reading

IN ORDER TO COMPLETE this book I relied on my own experience as well as the work of others. Even though there is a scarcity of good sources on the topic of gold production (especially in an easy-to-understand language), here are a few books that you should consider reading.

- *Gold Mining in the 21st Century* by Dave McCracken and Dave Mack
- *The Gold Book* by Pierre Lassonde
- *Gold Prospectors Handbook* by Jack Black
- *Advances in Gold Ore Processing* by Mike Adams and M.D. Adams
- *The Chemistry of Gold Extraction* by John Marsden and Iain House
- *Metallurgy of Gold* by Manuel Eissler
- *The Cyanide Handbook* by J.E. Clennell

In addition to these books, the following websites contain great information about gold production.

- Denvermineral.com
- Mine-Engineer.com
- Nevada-Outback-Gems.com
- Minerals.net
- GreatMining.com

Other Work

Other Work by this Author

GOLD PRODUCTION FROM BEGINNING to End is the third book by Mariusz Skonieczny. His other books are:
- *Why Are We So Clueless about the Stock Market*
- *The Basics of Understanding Financial Statements*

He also produced the Value Investing University DVD Collection, which consists of ten individual DVDs that teach investors how to find good stock picks, conduct due diligence, value companies, read financial statements, and much more.

Finally, he also publishes a monthly investment newsletter called Ultimate Value Finder. Every issue features three investment opportunities that he believes offer value to investors. The newsletter mainly focuses on small capitalization companies because small companies tend to be overlooked by investors, and therefore, they have a higher probability of being mispriced. However, at the same time, they are more volatile and risky.